WHAT
WAS IT

before it was a sweater?

by Roseva Shreckhise
illustrated by Helen Endres

THE CHILD'S WORLD

ELGIN, ILLINOIS 60120

Distributed by Childrens Press, 1224 West Van Buren Street, Chicago, Illinois 60607.

Library of Congress Cataloging in Publication Data

Shreckhise, Roseva, 1925-
  What was it before it was my sweater?

  (A Let's find out book)
  Summary: Traces the process by which wool is grown
on sheep, cut, sorted, cleaned, dyed, spun into yarn,
and knitted into sweaters. Includes directions for
making a lamb out of wool and felt.
  1. Sweaters—Juvenile literature. 2. Wool—
Juvenile literature. 3. Sheep—Juvenile literature.
[1. Wool. 2. Sweaters] I. Endres, Helen, ill.
II. Title. III. Series: Let's find out book.
TT680.S557 1985   677'.3132   85-11401
ISBN 0-89565-324-9

1 2 3 4 5 6 7 8 9 10 11 12 R 91 90 89 88 87 86 85

WHAT
WAS IT

before it was

a

sweater?

I just got a wool sweater for my birthday. It is so soft and warm! How did my sweater get to be a sweater, just right for me? What was it before it was a sweater?

Let's find out how wool sweaters are made and where the wool comes from!

It starts each year when little lambs
are born. Their wooly coats feel so
bumpy and curly!

The lambs' mothers take good care of
them. They nurse them. And they stay
beside them as they learn to eat grass.

A shepherd (or sheep herder) helps take care of the lambs. If a lamb gets hurt, he washes the hurt place and puts oil on it. The shepherd also makes sure the sheep have good grass and water. He knows that healthy sheep will have the very best wool.

Sometimes, sheep dogs help the
shepherd take care of the sheep.

For more than a year, the sheep eat and grow bigger and bigger. And as the time passes, their wool gets longer and thicker.

When their fleecy coats are several
inches thick, the sheep are ready for
a "haircut." This usually happens in late
spring. By then the weather has become
warm enough so that the sheep will not
catch cold when their coats are cut off.

A person called a sheep shearer gives the sheep their haircuts. He holds a sheep tightly, as he carefully cuts off the wool. The wool usually comes off in one large piece.

The sheep are glad to get their long, thick wool cut off before the hot, summer weather comes. And it will grow back before winter returns.

After the wool is cut off the sheep, it is sent to a factory. There it is sorted into bundles, according to length, thickness, or for other reasons.

After this, the wool is cleaned.

Then it may be dyed many
pretty colors.

Next, the wool is put between large rollers with rows of teeth like a comb. The rollers straighten out the wool—a little like combing your hair to get the tangles out.

Finally, large machines spin ropes of
wool into yarn . . .

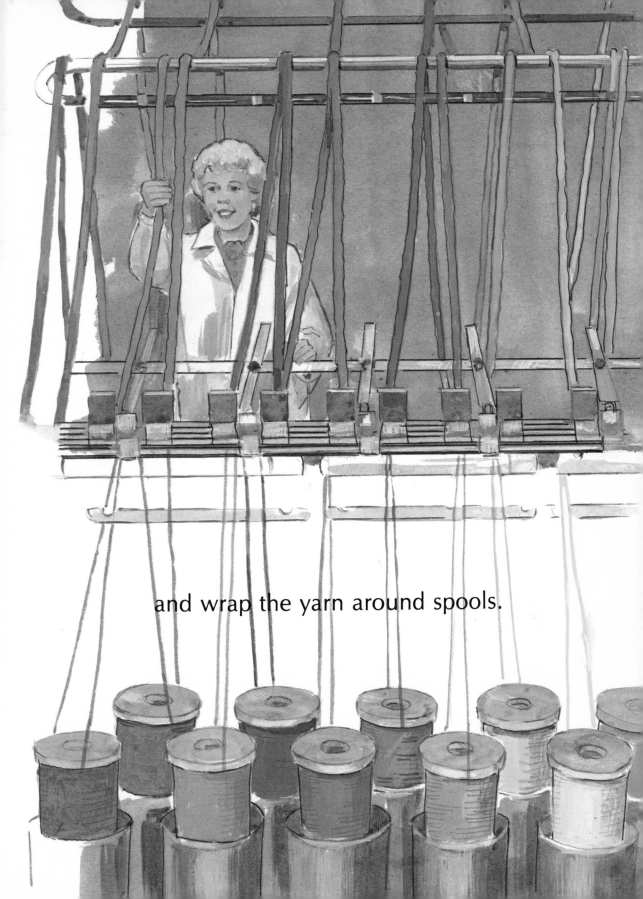

and wrap the yarn around spools.

Some yarn is sent to stores to be sold. Many people buy this yarn and make sweaters and scarves and mittens and many other things.

The spools of yarn are sent to knitting mills where sweaters and other things are made on knitting machines.

Sweaters, lots of sweaters, all different kinds of sweaters are made at knitting mills.

Then the sweaters are sent to large buildings called wholesale houses. . . and then to department stores. Some go to stores in big cities. Some go to stores in small towns.

My grandmother bought my sweater
at a store near her house.

So that is the story of what my
sweater was before it was a sweater.
Just think, a sheep born more than a
year ago has given me a pretty, new
sweater. And he has grown a new coat
for himself, so we will both be warm!

Next spring, someone will cut off his wool again. It may be made into a new sweater for some other lucky boy or girl. Maybe YOU!

Plus Pages

Here is the circle story you have read about how sweaters are made from the coats of wooly lambs!

6. Yarn is used to make sweaters.

5. Wool is made into yarn.

1. Little lambs are born.

2. Lambs grow wool.

3. Sheep are sheared.

4. Wool is cleaned and dyed.

You can make your own wooly lamb. Here's how:

←head

1. Cut two round pieces of lambs wool for the body. Cut one smaller piece for the head.

↖ body pieces ↗

2. From black felt, cut four legs, two ears, and one tail.

← legs   ← ears   ←tail

3. Glue the legs and tail to the skin side of the body piece. (To make a hanger, glue a looped piece of string to the top of the body piece, opposite the legs.)

← string loop hanger

4. Glue the body pieces together, skin sides touching.

5. Glue on the head piece.

6. On a small piece of white felt, draw a sheep face.

7. Glue the face to the head, and then glue on the ears.

Now you have a wooly lamb of your own! Next time you get a new wool sweater, think of the wooly lamb that gave up his coat to make your sweater.